The Ultimate Curry Cookbook

The Best Curry Recipes from All Corners of The World

BY: Allie Allen

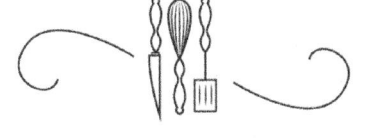

COOK & ENJOY

Copyright 2019 Allie Allen

Copyright Notes

This book is written as an informational tool. While the author has taken every precaution to ensure the accuracy of the information provided therein, the reader is warned that they assume all risk when following the content. The author will not be held responsible for any damages that may occur as a result of the readers' actions.

The author does not give permission to reproduce this book in any form, including but not limited to: print, social media posts, electronic copies or photocopies, unless permission is expressly given in writing.

My Gift to You for Buying My Book!

I would like to extend an exclusive offer to receive free and discounted eBooks every day! This special gift is my way of saying thanks. If you fill in the subscription box below you will begin to receive special offers directly to your email.

Not only that! You will also receive notifications letting you know when an offer will expire. You will never miss a chance to get a free book! Who wouldn't want that?

Fill in the subscriber information below and get started today!

SUBSCRIBE
YOUR E-MAIL ADRESS

https://allie-allen.getresponsepages.com/

Table of Contents

Popular Curry Recipes 7

1) Classic Curry Chicken with Potatoes 8

2) Fish Curry 11

3) Eggplant Curry 16

4) Spicy Malvani Chicken Curry 19

5) Indonesian Rendang Curry 23

6) Chicken Tikka Masala 26

7) Pumpkin Curry with Citrus 29

8) Butter Chicken 32

9) Thai Penang Curry 35

10) Lemon and Green Chili Chicken Curry 38

11) Thai Red Curry 41

12) Chicken Stew and Appam 44

13) Thai Green Chicken Curry 48

14) Kolhapuri Chicken 51

15) Black Eye Pea Ham and Collard Green Curry 54

16) Zucchini Tomato Curry 57

17) Prawns in Coconut Milk Curry 60

18) Tomato and Lentil Curry 63

19) Chicken Curry with Roasted Coconut and Spices 66

20) Vegetable Curry 70

21) Guyanese Goat Curry 73

22) Basil Chicken Curry fused with Coconut Ginger 76

23) Cauliflower Tomato Curry 80

24) Sweet and Spicy Green Apple Curry 83

25) Bhindi Masala 86

26) Chicken Xacuti 90

27) Crab Masala Fry 94

28) Chicken Do Pyaaza 97

29) Murg Rezala 101

30) Sali Marghi... 105

About the Author... 108

Author's Afterthoughts.. 110

Popular Curry Recipes

sssssssssssssssssssssssssssssssssssssssssssssss

1) Classic Curry Chicken with Potatoes

This recipe of curry chicken with potatoes can also be prepared on the stove. Simply simmer the mixture for 30 minutes instead of baking. You can adjust the quantity of cayenne, fish sauce and sugar according to your taste. Serve with lots of Thai jasmine rice.

Yield: 4-5

Cooking Time: 60 minutes

List of Ingredients:

- Chicken breast, 1 pound, cubed
- Potatoes, 3, cut into chunks
- Bay leaf, 1
- Cinnamon stick, 1
- Tomatoes, 2, diced
- Thai curry powder, 2 tbsp.
- Ketchup, 1 + ½ tbsp.
- Ginger, 1 piece
- Coriander, handful
- Chicken stock, ½ cup
- Garlic, 4 cloves, minced
- Shallots, 2, chopped
- Cayenne pepper, 1 tsp.
- Kaffir lime leaves, 2
- Fish sauce, 3 tbsp.
- Vegetable oil, 3 tbsp.
- Sugar, ½ tsp.
- Thick coconut milk, 1 can

ssssssssssssssssssssssssssssssssssssssssssssssss

Procedure:

Preheat the oven to 350 F.

Add curry powder, cayenne, bay leaf and cinnamon stick in a large pan. Roast the ingredients for 2 minutes until aromatic.

Add 2 tbsp. oil and add ginger, shallots and garlic. Add 3 tbsp. of chicken stock and stir fry for 1 minute.

Now add chicken cubes and potatoes. Fry for 1 minute and mix well.

Add chicken stock and ketchup. Combine well.

Stir coconut milk, sugar, and kaffir leaves and fish sauce. Combine well.

Transfer the mixture to a casserole and cover. Bake for 1 hour.

During the last 15 minutes add tomatoes.

Garnish with coriander leaves and serve.

2) Fish Curry

This recipe is also known as CHETTINADU MEEN KUZHAMBU. This recipe of fish curry requires the fish to be cooked off the flame in the curry. This way the fillets absorb more flavors from the spices and it makes the dish delicious.

Yield: 6

Cooking Time: 50 minutes

List of Ingredients:

For Marinade:

- Fish, 7
- Lemon juice, 1 tbsp.
- Turmeric powder, 1 tsp.
- Salt, 1 tbsp.

To Grind:

- Onions, 6 small, chopped
- Ginger, ½ inch
- Coconut, ¼ cup
- Tomato, 2 chopped
- Coriander seeds, 1 tbsp.
- Garlic, 4 cloves, minced
- Fennel seeds, 1 tsp.
- Poppy seeds, 1 tsp., soaked in water

For Tempering:

- Mustard seeds, 1 tsp.
- Chili powder, 1 tbsp.
- Fenugreek, 1 tsp.
- Tamarind, lemon sized soaked in ½ cup warm water and pulp extracted
- Curry leaves, 6
- Oil, 1 ½ tbsp.
- Garlic, 5 cloves, chopped
- Turmeric powder, 1 tsp.
- Asafetida, 1 pinch
- Red chili, 1
- Shallots, 5, chopped
- Coriander powder, 1 tbsp.
- Onion, 1 big, chopped

sssssssssssssssssssssssssssssssssssssssssssss

Procedure:

Combine all the ingredients of the marinade and rub evenly all over the fish fillets. Keep aside.

To prepare grinding mixture, sauté onions until translucent. Add tomato and cook for a few minutes.

Transfer the onion mixture to the mortar. Add all the remaining ingredients and form a fine paste. Set aside.

Temper mustard seeds in oil. Add curry leaves, red chili, fenugreek, garlic, asafetida and onions. Sauté for 5 minutes.

Now add the paste, coriander powder and chili powder. Sauté for 2 minutes.

Add tamarind pulp with 2 cups of water. Season with salt. Cook the mixture for 25 minutes so that it reaches its desired thickness.

Once the gravy releases its oil add fish fillets and boil for an additional 5 minutes.

Cover the lid and let the fillets stand in the heat for 30 minutes to be cooked itself.

Garnish with coriander leaves and serve.

3) Eggplant Curry

This recipe makes an Italian fusion eggplant curry that is loaded with spices. The highlighted ingredients in this recipe are anchovies, eggplant, vinegar, turmeric, chilies and milk. It can be served with rice.

Yield: 4

Cooking Time: 45 minutes

List of Ingredients:

- Eggplant, American style large, 2
- Red onion, 1, diced
- Salt, to taste
- Pepper, to taste
- Curry leaves, 10-15
- Green bell pepper, 1, sliced
- Cumin seeds, 1 tsp.
- Black mustard leaves, 1 tsp.
- Anchovy fillets, 1 can of 2 oz.
- Turmeric powder, ½ tsp.
- Apple cider vinegar, 1 tsp.
- Garlic, 1 tbsp., grated
- Red chili flakes, to taste
- Curry powder, 1 tsp.
- Milk, 1 cup

ssssssssssssssssssssssssssssssssssssssssssssssssss

Procedure:

Heat oil in a pan. Add anchovy along with its oil and cover the lid. When the anchovies have melted add mustard seeds, curry leaves, and cumin seeds. Temper for 30 seconds with lid on.

Add eggplant and cook for 10 minutes.

When the eggplants are cooked add onions, garlic and pepper. Cook for 5 minutes.

Add curry powder, salt, red chili, pepper and turmeric. Combine well and cook for 5 minutes.

Stir vinegar and milk. Cook again for 10 minutes.

Transfer to a serving bowl and serve.

4) Spicy Malvani Chicken Curry

This is a traditional malvani style chicken curry recipe made in a spicy coconut paste and delicious malvani masala. The chicken is cooked until it becomes tender and has absorbed all the spices well. You can serve it with homemade tortillas.

Yield: 8

Cooking Time: 1 hour

List of Ingredients:

- Chicken, 1 pound, cubed

For the curry:

- Water
- Coriander leaves, ½ bunch
- Onions, 3, chopped
- Coconut, handful, grated
- Oil, 3 tbsp.

For the malvani masala:

- Nutmeg, ½
- Turmeric powder, ½ tsp.
- Bay leaf, 1
- Cumin seeds, 1 tsp.
- Dry red chilies, 7
- Red chili powder, 1 tsp.
- Cloves, 7
- Coriander seeds, 1 tsp.
- Black peppercorns, 10
- Cinnamon stick, 1 large

For the coconut masala paste:

- Garlic, 6 cloves
- Ginger, ¾ inch
- Green chilies, 3
- Coconut, 1 grated

sssssssssssssssssssssssssssssssssssssssssssssss

Procedure:

In a small pan roast the ingredients of malvani masala. Toss well.

Transfer them in a food processor and grind coarsely. Keep aside.

Now process all the coconut masala ingredients into a paste.

Sauté onions in a large saucepan until translucent.

Add coconut paste and mix well. Cook for 10 minutes.

Add malvani masala and combine. Add salt and red chili powder to taste.

Add chicken and water. Combine well and cover the lid.

Cook on low heat for 40 minutes.

When chicken is tender and thick curry is formed, transfer to the serving dish and garnish with grated coconut and coriander leaves.

5) Indonesian Rendang Curry

Rendang curry is popular all around Indonesia. This recipe can also be made with beef. It's just that it is a little simple to make with chicken and takes comparatively less time. It goes well with Thai coconut rice.

Yield: 4

Cooking Time: 25 minutes

List of Ingredients:

- Chicken pieces, 1 pound

For the Curry Sauce:

- Coconut milk, ½ can
- Garlic, 4 cloves
- Ground coriander, 1 tbsp.
- Onion, 1, peeled and quartered
- Ground cumin, 1 tbsp.
- Lemongrass, 2 tbsp., chopped
- Ginger, 1 piece
- Red chilies, 3
- Tamarind paste, ¾ tbsp.
- Brown sugar, 1 tbsp.
- Turmeric, ½ tsp.
- Dark soy sauce, 2 tsp.
- Fish sauce, 4 tbsp.
- Cinnamon, 1 ½ tsp.
- Nutmeg, ¼ tsp.
- Shrimp paste, 1 tsp.
- Whole star anise, 2
- Cloves, ¼ tsp.

- Coriander leaves for garnishing

sssssssssssssssssssssssssssssssssssssssssssss

Procedure:

Grind all curry sauce ingredients into a fine paste except for anise.

Heat a wok over medium flame and add sauce.

Add chicken and star anise and mix well.

Bring the mixture to a boil while stirring occasionally.

Reduce the flame and simmer for 1 hour.

Transfer the mixture to serving bowl and garnish with coriander leaves.

Serve with Thai coconut rice.

6) Chicken Tikka Masala

This is a spicy and flavorful chicken curry recipe with creamy texture and wonderful flavors. The chicken is initially baked which lets it absorb the marinade well. It can be served with rice or nan.

Yield: 4

Cooking Time: 30 minutes

List of Ingredients:

- Tandoori paste, 2 tbsp.
- Olive oil, 3 tbsp.
- Chicken breasts, 2, skinned and chopped
- Onion, 1, peeled and chopped
- Tomatoes, 1 can 7oz.
- Yogurt, 2 tbsp.
- Bay leaves, 2
- Single cream, 3 tbsp.
- Ginger, 2 tbsp.
- Red chilies, 2. Seeded and chopped
- Garlic, 2 cloves, peeled and chopped
- Coriander leaves, handful
- Turmeric powder, ¼ tsp.
- Ground coriander, ½ tsp.
- Paprika, ¼ tsp.
- Garam masala, ¼ tsp.
- Ground cumin, ½ tsp.
- Salt, ¼ tsp.

sssssssssssssssssssssssssssssssssssssssssssssss

Procedure:

Combine tandoori paste with yogurt and massage evenly over the chicken. Refrigerate for 2 hours.

Preheat the oven to 350 F.

Assemble the marinated chicken on a baking sheet and bake for 10 minutes.

Combine cream with ginger, tomatoes and garlic and blend to form a paste. Keep aside.

Sauté onions and bay leaf until onions turn golden brown. Add paprika, garam masala, turmeric, coriander, chilies, salt and cumin. Combine and cook for 2 minutes.

Add chicken and cook for 5 minutes.

Now stir cream mixture and tomatoes. Cover the lid and cook for 10 minutes.

Add a little water and cook until combined.

Transfer to a serving bowl and garnish with coriander.

7) Pumpkin Curry with Citrus

This recipe of pumpkin curry is made with colorful vegetables and flavorful spices. The mild sweetness of pumpkin blends wonderfully with exotic spices and lime juice. Serve with rice.

Yield: 4

Cooking Time: 30 minutes

List of Ingredients:

- Small pumpkin, ½
- Medium carrots, 2, julienned
- Chick peas, ½ can, drained
- Yellow bell pepper, 1, cut into small pieces
- Yam, 1 small, peeled and cubed
- Orange rind, 2 tbsp., grated
- Cherry tomatoes, 1 cup

For the Curry Sauce:

- Thai chili sauce, 2 tsp.
- Turmeric, ½ tsp.
- Lime juice, ½
- Soy sauce, 2 + ½ tbsp.
- Garlic, 4 cloves
- Coconut milk, 1 can
- Tamarind paste, 1 tsp.
- Basil leaves, handful
- Ground coriander seeds, 1 tbsp.
- Fennel seeds, 1 tsp.
- Brown sugar, 1 tbsp.
- Orange juice, 1

- Purple onions, 1/3 sliced
- Rice vinegar, 1 tbsp.
- Roasted pumpkin seeds, 1 tbsp.

sssssssssssssssssssssssssssssssssssssssssssssss

Procedure:

Process all the curry paste ingredients together in a blender into a fine paste.

Scoop out the seeds from pumpkin and slice them in cubes.

Mix pumpkin with carrots, curry sauce and yam and cook over medium flame.

Once the sauce starts boiling, reduce the flame and simmer for 10 minutes while stirring occasionally.

Add bell peppers, orange rind, tomatoes and chick peas. Mix well and simmer for another 5 minutes.

Transfer to a serving bowl and garnish with pumpkin seeds and basil leaves.

8) Butter Chicken

This recipe makes flavorsome butter chicken with lots of spices and chilies to give it a strong spicy taste. The chicken is marinated overnight for enhanced flavor. It can be served with rice or nan.

Yield: 4

Cooking Time: 30 minutes

List of Ingredients:

- Chicken, 700 g

For marinade:

- Curd, 1 ½ cups
- Red chili powder, 1 tsp.
- Salt, to taste
- Ginger and garlic paste, 1 tsp.

For the gravy:

- White butter, 175 g
- Red chili powder, 1 tsp.
- Crushed fenugreek leaves, ½ tsp.
- Black cumin seeds, ½ tsp.
- Fresh cream, 100 g
- Tomatoes, ½ kg, purred
- Salt, to taste
- Sugar, ½ tsp.
- Green chilies, 4, sliced

sssssssssssssssssssssssssssssssssssssssssssssss

Procedure:

Combine curd with chili powder, salt, ginger and garlic paste.

Rub the paste over the chicken and refrigerate overnight.

Bake the chicken for 10 minutes in an oven.

For gravy, melt butter in a saucepan and add tomato puree, salt, sugar, cumin seeds and red chili. Combine well.

Transfer chicken to saucepan and add fenugreek leaves, cream and green chilies. Cook until chicken is tender.

Serve hot.

9) Thai Penang Curry

This recipe makes authentic Thai Penang curry filled with distinct flavors of Burma, Malaysia and India. This recipe can also be prepared on your stove. Serve it with plenty of Thai jasmine rice.

Yield: 4

Cooking Time: 60 minutes

List of Ingredients:

- Chicken cubes, 1 pound
- Kaffir lime leaves, 2
- Tomatoes, 3, cut into wedges
- Fresh basil leaves, ½ cup
- Red bell pepper, 1, sliced

For the Curry Sauce:

- Tomato paste, 4 tbsp.
- Paprika, 1 tbsp.
- Garlic, 3 cloves
- Turmeric, ½ tsp.
- Soy sauce, 1 tbsp.
- Fish sauce, 2 tbsp.
- Dark soy sauce, ½ tsp.
- Whole cumin, ½ tsp.
- Onion, 1, quartered
- Red chili, 2, minced
- Cinnamon, ½ tsp.
- Ground coriander, ½ tsp.
- Chili powder, 1 tbsp.
- Shrimp paste, 1 tsp.

- Ginger, 1 piece, sliced
- Lime juice, ½
- Ground clove, 1/8 tsp.
- Nutmeg, 1/8 tsp.
- Coconut milk, 1 can

sssssssssssssssssssssssssssssssssssssssssssssss

Procedure:

Preheat the oven to 375 F.

To prepare curry sauce, process all the curry sauce ingredients in a blender except for whole cumin seeds. Process into a fine paste.

Spread the sauce evenly on a casserole dish and assemble chicken cubes and cumin seeds. Sprinkle lime leaves and mix.

Bake for 45 minutes.

Now add bell peppers and tomatoes and bake for an additional 20 minutes.

Garnish with basil leaves and serve.

10) Lemon and Green Chili Chicken Curry

This curry recipe is made with a great blend of flavors. Chicken cooked in lemon and green chilies gives a strong, spicy and citrusy mix of flavors. It can be served with nan or rice.

Yield: 4

Cooking Time: 40 minutes

List of Ingredients:

- Chicken, 1 g, cubed
- Green chilies, 4, slit
- Onions, 200 g, blanched and pureed
- Fresh cream, 50 ml
- Turmeric powder, 1 tsp.
- Ginger garlic paste, 1 tsp.
- Fenugreek seeds, 1 pinch
- Yogurt, 2 cups
- Malt vinegar, 2 tsp.
- Coriander powder, 1 tbsp.
- Turmeric powder, 1 tsp.
- Lemon pickle, 100 g
- Yellow chili powder, 1 tsp.
- Fresh coriander for garnishing
- Ghee, 100 ml

sssssssssssssssssssssssssssssssssssssssssssss

Procedure:

Melt ghee and stir fry ginger and garlic paste.

Add onion puree and mix. Cook for 2 minutes.

Add chicken and mix well. Now add garam masala, turmeric powder, yellow chili powder, salt, and yogurt and coriander powder. Combine well and cook until thick gravy forms.

Stir vinegar and lemon pickle and combine well.

Add green chilies, fenugreek seeds and cream. Combine well and transfer to the serving bowl. Garnish with coriander leaves.

11) Thai Red Curry

Thai red curry is a spicy and scrumptious dish served with rice. Red curry paste is very simple to prepare, all you have to do is combine the ingredients and grind them well. You can use more or less spices according to your taste. Lime juice and coconut milk are used to bring down the hot flavor a little.

Yield: 4

Cooking Time: 60 minutes

List of Ingredients:

- Chicken breast, 1 pound, cubed
- Kaffir lime leaves, 2
- Fresh basil, handful
- Coriander, handful
- Eggplant, 1 cup, chopped
- Red bell pepper, 1, chopped
- Cinnamon stick, ½
- Tomatoes, 2, diced

For Red Curry Sauce:

- Coconut milk, 1 can
- Garlic, 4 cloves, chopped
- Ground cumin, ½ tsp.
- Fresh lime juice, 2 tbsp.
- Ginger, 1 piece, grated
- Lemongrass, 3 tbsp., minced
- Shrimp paste, 1 tsp.
- Tomato puree, 2 tbsp.
- Shallot, 1, chopped
- Brown sugar, 1 tbsp.
- Ground coriander, ½ tsp.

- Chili powder, 2 tbsp.
- Cayenne pepper, 1 tsp.
- Fish sauce, 2 tbsp.

sssssssssssssssssssssssssssssssssssssssssssssss

Procedure:

Preheat the oven to 350 F.

Assemble the chicken cubes on a casserole dish.

Process all curry sauce ingredients in a blender until smooth. Spread the sauce over chicken cubes.

Add eggplant, kaffir leaves and cinnamon stick. Cover the dish and bake for 45 minutes.

Now add tomatoes and bell peppers and mix well with the sauce.

Bake for an additional 20 minutes or until vegetables and chicken have cooked through.

Transfer the curry in to the serving bowl and garnish with basil and coriander leaves.

Serve.

12) Chicken Stew and Appam

Chicken stew and appam are the specialties of Kerala. Appam is a rice version of pancakes. Chicken, tomatoes and potatoes are cooked in coconut milk with red and green chilies to add the spice to it.

Yield: 3

Cooking Time: 1 hour

List of Ingredients:

For chicken stew:

- Chicken, ½ kg
- Red chili, 1, chopped
- Coconut milk, 1st and 2nd extract from 1 coconut
- Coconut oil, 4 tbsp.
- Lemon, 1
- Green chilies, 2, chopped
- Onions, 2 finely chopped
- Salt, to taste
- Coriander, small bunch
- Ginger garlic paste, 1 tbsp.
- Potatoes, 2, diced
- Tomatoes, 2, chopped
- Pepper, to taste

For the appam:

- Rice, 1 cup, soaked in water
- Coconut, 3 tbsp., grated
- Sugar, 1 tbsp.
- Baking soda, ½ tsp.
- Salt, ½ tsp.
- Rice, 1 tbsp., cooked

sssssssssssssssssssssssssssssssssssssssssssssss

Procedure:

Sauté onion in coconut oil. Add chilies and ginger garlic paste. Stir fry until golden.

Add chicken and cook for 3 minutes.

Now add potatoes and tomatoes. Combine well.

Stir 2nd extract coconut milk and water.

Season with salt and pepper. Cover the lid and cook on low flame for 45 minutes.

When the chicken is cooked, stir 1st extract, lemon juice and garnish with coriander.

Now to prepare appam, process soaked rice, cooked rice and grated coconut together into a thick paste. Transfer to a bowl and keep overnight.

Now add salt, baking soda, water and sugar in the fermented mixture and process again to form a paste.

Spread 1 heaping scoop of appam mixture in a pan and cover. Cook for 2 minutes or until the edges are brown.

Serve with curry.

13) Thai Green Chicken Curry

This recipe makes a flavorsome curry in Thai style with Thai sauce and some very basic ingredients. Do not leave the kaffir lime leaves and basil leaves for too long otherwise they will lose their color. Serve with boiled rice.

Yield: 6

Cooking Time: 40 minutes

List of Ingredients:

- Potatoes, 225 g, cut into chunks
- Green beans, 100 g, trimmed and halved
- Caster sugar, 1 tsp.
- Fresh kaffir lime leaves, 2, shredded
- Basil leaves, handful
- Garlic, 1 clove, chopped
- Chicken breast, 450 g, cubed
- Thai fish sauce, 2 tsp.
- Vegetable oil, 1 tbsp.
- Coconut milk, 1 can of 40 ml
- Thai green curry, 4 tsp.

sssssssssssssssssssssssssssssssssssssssssssssss

Procedure:

Boil potatoes for 10 minutes. Add beans in the same boiling water and boil for another 5 minutes. Make sure potatoes and beans are not too soft just tender.

Heat oil and sauté garlic for 5-10 seconds. Add curry paste and stir for 10 seconds.

Stir coconut milk and let it boil slightly.

Add sugar, chicken and fish sauce and stir well.

Reduce the flame and cover the lid. Simmer for 10 minutes or until the chicken is cooked through.

Now add beans and potatoes and cook for 5 minutes. Add kaffir lime leaves. Add basil leaves and cook for 1 minute.

Serve immediately.

14) Kolhapuri Chicken

Kolhapuri chicken curry is marinated with lime juice, chilies, yogurt and turmeric. The masala is tempered until aromatic and then pureed. The spices used in this recipe are simple yet bring out an extraordinary flavor. It is best served with cooked rice.

Yield: 8

Cooking Time: 1 hour 40 minutes

List of Ingredients:

For marinade:

- Chicken, 1 kg
- Lime juice, 1 tsp.
- Yogurt, 2/3 cup
- Salt (sprinkle)
- Turmeric powder, 1 tsp.
- Red chili, 2 tsp.
- Garlic paste, 1 tsp.

For the kohlapur masala:

- Black pepper, ½ tsp.
- Tomato, 1 large, chopped
- Peanut/corn oil, 2 tsp.
- Onions, 2 medium, chopped
- Coconut, 2 tsp., grated
- Cinnamon sticks, 2
- Bay leaf, 1
- Cloves, 6
- Oil, 2 tsp.
- Coriander leaves, 1 tsp.

sss

Procedure:

Combine yogurt with all the marinade spices. Rub the paste evenly all over the chicken and set aside for 30 minutes.

Meanwhile sauté onions with bay leaf, cloves, black pepper and cinnamon. When the onions are done add grated coconut and sauté again for a few minutes.

Add tomatoes and cook for 10 minutes.

Keep the masala at room temperature. Puree it in a food processor and keep aside.

Heat oil and cook chicken for 25 minutes on low flame.

Add kohlapur masala paste and combine well. Cook for additional 5 minutes.

Garnish with coriander leaves and serve.

15) Black Eye Pea Ham and Collard Green Curry

This recipe is a great way to utilize some leftover ham from last night. You just have to grab the cans of black eyed peas, coconut milk, and tomatoes with chilies and season with some basic spices and you are done.

Yield: 4

Cooking Time: 55 minutes

List of Ingredients:

- Black eyed peas, 2 cans of 15 oz. rinsed
- Onion, 1, chopped
- Ham, 1 pound, cooked, chopped
- Green chilies, 4
- Cinnamon, 1 small stick
- Water
- Curry leaves, 15-20
- Collard greens, 11 bunch, stems removed, chopped
- Cumin seeds, 2 tsp.
- Coconut milk, 1 can of 15 oz.
- Black mustard seeds, 2 tsp.
- Salt, to taste
- Pepper, to taste
- Vinegar, 1 tsp.
- Garlic, 2 cloves, grated
- Ginger, 1 inch piece, grated
- Ground turmeric, ½ tsp.
- Curry powder, 2 tsp.
- Sugar, 1 tsp.
- Red chili flakes, to taste
- Red chili powder, to taste
- Tomatoes, 1 can of 15 oz. diced

- Fenugreek seeds, ½ tsp.

ssssssssssssssssssssssssssssssssssssssssssssss

Procedure:

Heat 2 tbsp. of oil and temper curry leaves, fenugreek seeds, mustard seeds, cinnamon stick and cumin seeds for 30 seconds.

Add onions and chilies and cook for 5 minutes. Add ginger and garlic paste and cook for 1 minute.

Add collard greens and cook for 5 minutes. Season with turmeric, chili powder and curry powder. Cook for an additional 3 minutes.

Now add ham, tomatoes, sugar, vinegar and water. Cook for 5 minutes.

Add peas and simmer for 20 minutes. Lastly stir coconut milk and simmer for an additional 5 minutes.

Serve hot.

16) Zucchini Tomato Curry

This recipe makes a crispy zucchini in thick and spicy tomato sauce. Make sure you melt anchovies first before adding spices. Zucchini tomato curry can be served with rice.

Yield: 4

Cooking Time: 40 minutes

List of Ingredients:

- Zucchini, 4-6, medium size, sliced into 1 inch half moons
- Green chilies, 3, chopped
- Fenugreek seeds, 1 tsp.
- Ripe tomatoes, 4-6, large and cubed
- Black mustard seeds, 1 tsp.
- Anchovy fillets, 1 can of 2 oz. in olive oil
- Cumin seeds, 1 tsp.
- Salt, to taste
- Pepper, to taste
- Ginger, 1 tbsp., grated
- Curry leaves, 12
- Turmeric powder, ½ tsp.
- Garlic, 1 tbsp., grated
- Onion, 1 medium, sliced
- Sugar, 1 tsp.
- Red chili flakes, to taste

ssssssssssssssssssssssssssssssssssssssssssssss

Procedure:

Heat 2 tbsp. of oil.

Melt anchovies on medium flame. Add cumin seeds, curry leaves, fenugreek seeds and mustard seeds and temper for 1 minute.

Now add onions, ginger, chilies and garlic. Sauté for 3 minutes.

Add zucchini and season with pepper flakes, salt, turmeric and pepper. Stir fry for 3 minutes.

Now add tomatoes and combine well. Cook for 15-20 minutes or until zucchini is tender and a thick tomato gravy has formed.

Transfer to a serving bowl and serve.

17) Prawns in Coconut Milk Curry

This recipe of prawns is prepared in coconut milk gravy. The gravy is prepared by mixing onions and tomatoes with different seasoning and cooking until they infuse in flavor. Prawns do not require long cooking time so make sure you do not overcook them.

Yield: 4

Cooking Time: 50 minutes

List of Ingredients:

- Prawns, 400 g, deveined and washed
- Dried red chilies, 2
- Black pepper, ¼ tsp.
- Oil, 3 tbsp.
- Green chilies, 2, slit into half
- Turmeric powder, ½ tsp.
- Onion, 1 cup, chopped
- Salt, to taste
- Coriander powder, 2 tsp.
- Curry leaves, 2 sprigs
- Red chili powder, ½ tsp.
- Tomato, ½ cup, chopped
- Coconut milk, 1 cup
- Ginger garlic paste, 2 tsp.

sssssssssssssssssssssssssssssssssssssssssssss

Procedure:

Heat oil in a medium pan and temper curry leaves for 1 minute.

Add onions and sauté until translucent.

Add chilies and cook for 2 minutes.

Add ginger garlic paste and cook for 2 minutes.

Now add tomatoes with ½ cup water and cook for 3 minutes.

Season with coriander powder, salt, red chili powder, black pepper and turmeric powder. Add ½ cup water again and cook for 5 minutes.

Add coconut milk and bring to a boil. Reduce the flame and simmer for 3 minutes.

Add prawns and cook for 5-10 minutes.

Transfer to a serving bowl and garnish with coriander leaves.

18) Tomato and Lentil Curry

Tomato and lentil curry is made with mild spices and makes a perfect lunch in summer. This recipe is purely vegan so if you are cutting down on meat you can try this out and enjoy it with rice.

Yield: 4

Cooking Time: 55 minutes

List of Ingredients:

- Orange lentils, 2 cups, rinsed well
- Cumin seeds, 1 tbsp.
- Ginger, 1 tbsp., grated
- Turmeric powder, ½ tsp.
- Cumin powder, 1 tsp.
- Water, 3-4 cups
- Green chilies, 2, chopped
- Cinnamon stick, ½ inch small
- Fresh tomatoes, 4 cups, chopped
- Onions, 1, diced
- Salt, to taste
- Curry leaves, 10-15
- Red chili flakes, to taste
- Garlic, 2-3 cloves, minced
- Coconut milk, ½ cup
- Mustard seeds, ½ tbsp.

sssssssssssssssssssssssssssssssssssssssssssss

Procedure:

Boil lentils in water, turmeric and cinnamon stick for 25 minutes or until the lentils are so tender that they easily mash.

Meanwhile temper cumin seeds, mustard seeds and curry leaves in a pan. Add onions, garlic, chili and ginger. Sauté for 2 minutes.

Now add tomatoes and season with chili powder, cumin powder and salt. Cook for 12 minutes.

Now add lentils in the gravy and combine well. Add coconut milk and mix again. Cook for 5-7 minutes then transfer to a serving bowl.

19) Chicken Curry with Roasted Coconut and Spices

This recipe is Kerala's specialty and is mostly served at weddings. The recipe needs elaborate cooking as the spices are first roasted and then blended. Roasting the ingredients may seem like a lot of work but it enhances the flavors of the dish incredibly.

Yield: 6

Cooking Time: 65 minutes

List of Ingredients:

For the Coconut Masala Paste:

- Shallots, 15
- Mustard seeds, 2 tsp.
- Cardamom, 1
- Dried red chilies, 10
- Water
- Heaped chili powder, 1 tsp.
- Pepper corns, 3
- Heaped coriander powder, 2 tsp.
- Coconut, ¾ cup, grated
- Turmeric powder, ½ tsp.
- Cumin seeds, ¾ tsp.
- Cinnamon, 4 cloves
- Fennel seeds, 1 tsp.
- Fenugreek seeds, 1 pinch
- For the Chicken Curry:
- Chicken, 1 pound
- Onion, 2 large, sliced
- Coconut oil, 3 tbsp.
- Turmeric powder, ½ tsp.
- Salt, to taste

- Garlic, 2 tsp., chopped
- Tomatoes, 2 large, chopped
- Curry leaves, 1 sprig
- Ginger, 2 tsp., chopped

For Tempering:

- Mustard seeds, 1 tsp.
- Green chilies, 2, cut lengthwise
- Coconut oil, 3 tbsp.
- Curry leaves, 5-7
- Shallots, 4, sliced
- Dried red chilies, 4
- Vinegar, 1 ½ tsp.

ssssssssssssssssssssssssssssssssssssssssssssssss

Procedure:

Roast red chilies until it turns slightly black and keep aside.

Roast shallots and keep aside.

Heat coconut oil and add all the spices and sauté until coconut turns brown.

Grind coconut with shallots, dried chilies and spices. Add water as required to form a paste. Keep the mixture aside.

Temper garlic, curry leaves and ginger for 5 minutes.

Add onions and sauté until soft.

Now add tomatoes and sauté for 5 minutes more.

Add chicken and combine well. Cook for 3 minutes.

Add coconut paste, salt and water. Combine well and cover the lid. Cook until the gravy forms and the chicken is cooked through.

For tempering heat oil and add mustard seeds. When the seeds start to splutter add red chilies, shallots and green chilies. Stir fry.

Now add curry leaves and for 1 minute.

Spread this over the cooked chicken and add vinegar.

Serve with rice.

20) Vegetable Curry

This is another pure vegan curry recipe made with zucchini, mushrooms, corn, bell pepper and tomatoes. Make sure you check the seasoning for salt because vegetables have the tendency to absorb salt. It is best served with rice.

Yield: 4

Cooking Time: 50 minutes

List of Ingredients:

- Fresh corn, 2 cups
- Zucchini, 2-3, cut into large pieces
- Button mushrooms, ½ pound, sliced
- Green bell peppers, 1 large, chopped
- Tomatoes, 2-3 large, chopped in to large pieces
- Coconut milk, 6 oz.
- Mustard seeds, 1 tsp.
- Curry leaves, 15-20
- Water, ¼ cup
- Red chili flakes, to taste
- Cinnamon stick, 1
- Green chilies, 2, seeded and chopped
- Curry powder, 2 tsp.
- Cumin powder, 1 tsp.
- Salt, to taste
- Fenugreek seeds, 1 tsp.
- Turmeric powder, ½ tsp.
- Ginger, 1 inch piece, grated
- Garlic, 2 cloves minced

ssssssssssssssssssssssssssssssssssssssssssssssss

Procedure:

Temper curry leaves, mustard seeds, cinnamon stick, cumin seeds and fenugreek seeds in 1 tbsp. canola oil.

Add garlic and ginger. Sauté for 30 seconds.

Add mushrooms and sauté until brown.

Add zucchini and stir fry for 5 minutes. Add tomatoes and cook for 5 minutes.

Season with chili flakes, cumin powder, turmeric, salt and curry powder. Cook for another 5 minutes.

Add corn and bell pepper. Add water and cook for 15 minutes. Stir a few times to combine.

Add coconut milk and reduce the flame. Simmer for 5 minutes. Give the gravy a good stir and dish out.

21) Guyanese Goat Curry

Goat meat contains less fat than lean meat or pork. The meat is juicy and makes delicious soup, stew and curry. Let your meat cook for enough time so it becomes fork tender. Serve it with a lot of rice to enjoy every bite.

Yield: 4

Cooking Time: 60 minutes

List of Ingredients:

- Goat meat, 2 ½ pounds
- Cumin seeds, 2 tsp.
- Cloves, ½ tsp.
- Garlic, 3 cloves, minced
- Allspice, ½ tsp.
- Fenugreek seeds, 2 tsp.
- Fennel seeds, 1 tsp.
- Onion, 1, chopped
- Mustard seeds, 1 tsp.
- Black peppercorns, 1 tsp.
- Coriander seeds, 2 tsp.
- Ground turmeric, 2 tsp.
- Lemon, 1
- Oil, 2 tbsp.

sssssssssssssssssssssssssssssssssssssssssssssss

Procedure:

Toast the all the spices except for turmeric. Toast for 3 minutes.

Remove the spices from the pan and add turmeric in the same pan and stir.

Grind the toasted spiced finely.

Puree onions with garlic and form a thick paste. Add water if needed.

Combine onion-garlic paste with toasted spices and turmeric together into a paste.

Heat oil and add the spice mixture and cook for 30 seconds.

Now add goat meat and combine. Cook for 2-3 minutes.

Add water and cover the lid. Boil the mixture.

Now reduce the flame and simmer for 2 ½ hours or until tender.

Remove the fat from the broth using a large spoon.

Serve with rice.

22) Basil Chicken Curry fused with Coconut Ginger

This recipe is very light and tastes delicious. The chicken is cooked in coconut milk, basil, zucchini, bell peppers and corns. It is served with a blend of jalapeno and mango which adds extra flavor to this curry. It is best served with naan.

Yield: 4

Cooking Time: 30 minutes

List of Ingredients:

- Lime Rice Basil Coconut Ginger:
- Coconut milk, 1 can of 14 oz.
- Lime, 1, juice + zest
- Basmati rice, 1 cup
- Fresh basil, 2 tbsp., chopped
- Ginger, 1 tbsp., grated

For Curry:

- Boneless Chicken, 1 pound, and cubed
- Ginger, 1 tbsp., grated
- Garlic, 2 cloves, minced
- Bell peppers, 2, chopped
- Jalapeno, 1, seeded and diced
- Thai red curry paste, 3 tbsp.
- Corns, 2 cups
- Coconut milk, 1 can of 14 oz.
- Goat cheese, 4 oz. crumbled
- Zucchini, 1, chopped
- Olive oil, 2 tbsp.
- Mango, 1, diced
- Fish sauce, 1 tbsp.

- Spicy curry powder, 1 tbsp.
- Fresh basil, ½ cup, chopped
- Cilantro, ¼ cup, chopped

ssssssssssssssssssssssssssssssssssssssssssssssss

Procedure:

To prepare rice, boil coconut milk and add rice with 1 tbsp. coconut oil, ginger and salt. Combine well and cover the lid. Keep the flame low and simmer for 10 minutes. After 10 minutes turn off the flame but do not uncover the lid or remove it from the saucepan from the stove for 20 minutes.

After 20 minutes add basil, zest and lime juice. Use a fork to slightly mix.

'To prepare curry, heat olive oil and cook chicken until golden brown. Transfer the chicken on a paper towel and keep aside.

Add 1 tbsp. of olive oil and sauté corn and red peppers for 3 minutes.

Add zucchini, garlic, and ginger. Sauté until the zucchini is tender.

Bring back the chicken to cooked vegetables and toss well.

Season with curry powder and curry paste and cook for 2 minutes.

Stir fish sauce and coconut milk cook until a thick gravy forms.

Remove the saucepan from the stove and add cilantro and basil.

Combine jalapeno with mango. Serve with curry and garnish with cheese.

23) Cauliflower Tomato Curry

Cauliflower tomato curry recipe makes its own all spice powder. If you like your food extra hot then you can use 2 small Kashmiri chilies but do not use more otherwise your taste buds will be on fire. Serve the curry with cooked rice.

Yield: 4

Cooking Time: 55 minutes

List of Ingredients:

- Cauliflower, 250 g, chopped
- Tamarind extract, 50 ml
- Onion, chopped
- Coriander leaves, handful
- Ginger, 1 inch piece, sliced
- Coconut, 2 tbsp., desiccated
- Green chilies, 2, chopped
- Tomatoes, 250 g, pureed
- Salt, to taste
- Turmeric powder, ¼ tsp.
- Curry leaves, 5-10
- Vegetable stock, 125 ml
- Garlic, 2 cloves, minced
- Oil, 3 tbsp.
- Mustard seeds, 1 tsp.

For Masala Powder:

- Coriander seeds, ½ tsp.
- Kashmiri dry red chili, 1 small
- Fennel seeds. ½ tsp.
- Cumin seeds, ½ tsp.

Procedure:

Roast all the ingredients of masala powder and grind them for 30 seconds and form a fine powder and set aside.

Grind half onions with garlic, green chilies and ginger. Make a fine paste.

Sauté remaining onions until golden and add masala powder, mustard seeds, curry leaves and turmeric powder. Stir fry the mixture for 2 minutes.

Now add tomato puree with water, coconut and tamarind extract and bring the mixture to a boil.

Add cauliflower and turn the flame low letting the mixture simmer for 10 minutes or until cauliflower is cooked.

Transfer to the serving plate and garnish with coriander leaves.

24) Sweet and Spicy Green Apple Curry

This is a sweet and spicy curry recipe of apples cooked in different spices. The sweet and sour flavor of apples when combined with curry powder and coconut milk make an irresistible savory meal.

Yield: 4

Cooking Time: 45 minutes

List of Ingredients:

- Granny smith apples, 2 large, quartered
- Turmeric powder, ¼ tsp.
- Oil, 3 tbsp.
- Onion, ½ medium, sliced
- Roasted Sir Lankan curry powder, 1 ½ tbsp.
- Apple cider, 1/3 cup
- Garlic, 1 clove, chopped
- Mustard seeds, 1 ½ tsp.
- Jalapeno, 1, chopped
- Coconut milk, 3 tbsp.
- Chili powder, 1 tsp.
- Brown sugar, 2 tbsp.
- Dried red chili, 2, chopped

ssssssssssssssssssssssssssssssssssssssssssssssss

Procedure:

Preheat the oven to 350 F.

Heat oil in an ovenproof saucepan and add onions, mustard seeds, red chili and jalapeno and sauté until tender.

Add chili powder and curry powder. Mix well and cook for 30 seconds.

Add apples and season with salt, garlic and sugar. Cook for 5-7 minutes while stirring occasionally.

Now pop the dish in the oven and bake for 15 minutes.

Stir coconut milk and water. Place it back in the oven for 10 minutes.

Stir well before serving.

25) Bhindi Masala

Bhindi is known as okra. This recipe makes spicy fried okra curry. For the crispiness of okras, fry them separately and then add them to the gravy. They are best served with parathas and naans.

Yield: 4

Cooking Time: 50 minutes

List of Ingredients:

For Tomato Paste:

- Tomatoes, 3 Chopped
- Mace, 1 single strand
- Garlic, 4 cloves, chopped
- Green cardamom, 1
- Ginger, ½ inch piece
- Cloves, 2
- Cinnamon stick, ½ inch
- Yogurt, 2 tbsp.
- Green chilies, 2

For Okra:

- Okra, 250 g
- Coriander powder, ½ tsp.
- Cumin powder, ½ tsp.
- Fenugreek leaves, ½ tsp., crushed
- Red chili powder, ½ tsp.
- Bay leaf, 1
- Onions, ½ cup, chopped
- Coriander leaves, 2 tbsp., chopped
- Turmeric powder, ¼ tsp.
- Salt, to taste
- Oil, 4 tbsp., divided

sssssssssssssssssssssssssssssssssssssssssssssss

Procedure:

Chop okra into small pieces and set aside.

Grind all tomato paste ingredients together and keep it aside covered.

Heat 2 tbsp. of oil and sauté okra until cooked and browned. Transfer the fried okra in a plate and keep aside.

Add remaining oil in the same pan and temper bay leaf for 10 seconds.

Add onions and sauté until brown.

Reduce the flame and add the dry spices. Now add tomato paste and stir well.

Reduce the flame and cook the mixture until it starts releasing oil.

Stir ¾ cup water and add salt.

Now add fried okra and combine well.

Simmer the mixture for 6 minutes. Add fenugreek leaves and coriander leaves and give it a good stir.

Transfer to a serving bowl and serve.

26) Chicken Xacuti

This recipe of chicken xacuti is best for those who like super spicy food. The recipe uses traditional spices like coconut, poppy seeds, Kashmiri chilies, peppercorns, cashews and green chilies. It is best served with rice or Nan.

Yield: 4-5

Cooking Time: 30 minutes

List of Ingredients:

For the Chicken:

- Chicken, 1 pound
- Bay leaves, 2
- Salt, to taste
- Oil, 4 tbsp.
- Onion, 1, chopped

For the curry paste:

- Black peppercorns, 4
- Cinnamon stick, 1
- Kashmiri chilies, 6, seeded
- Garlic, 8 cloves, chopped
- Coriander seeds, 1 tsp.
- Oil, 2 tbsp.
- Onion, 1, chopped
- Cumin seeds, 2 tsp.
- Cloves, 4
- Long green chilies, 3, chopped

For the Coconut Paste:

- Unsalted cashews, ¼ cup
- Unsweetened coconut, ½ cup, grated
- Oil, 2 tbsp.
- White poppy seeds, 2 tsp.
- Water

sssssssssssssssssssssssssssssssssssssssssssssss

Procedure:

To make curry paste temper peppercorns, cinnamon, Kashmiri chilies, cloves, cumin seeds and coriander seeds. Add onions and sauté until caramelized.

When the mixture cools down a little blend it with water, garlic paste, green chilies and ginger in a food processor. Make a smooth paste.

To make coconut paste toast cashews, coconut and poppy seeds in oil until golden. Transfer the contents in a food processor and add a few drops of water. Process into a fine paste.

To prepare chicken, sauté bay leaves for 30 seconds. Add onions and cook until translucent.

Add curry paste and cook while stirring continuously. When the mixture releases its oil, increase the flame and add chicken. Combine well.

Add 1 cup water and cover the lid. Reduce the flame and simmer for 15 minutes.

Lastly add coconut paste and ½ cup water. Cook for 5-6 minutes. Sprinkle with salt.

Refrigerate overnight.

Reheat and serve next day with boiled rice.

27) Crab Masala Fry

This is sweet and spicy crab recipe loaded with spices. Crab meat is cooked in tomato puree while it absorbs the flavors of all spices. This recipe is best served with bread or boiled rice.

Yield: 2

Cooking Time: 50 minutes

List of Ingredients:

- Dungeness/Jonah crabs, 2 medium, halved
- Vegetable oil, 3 tbsp., divided
- Turmeric powder, 1 tsp.
- Tomato puree, 1 cup
- Dried red chili, 1
- Fennel seeds, 1 tsp.
- Cilantro leaves, 2 tbsp., finely chopped
- Onion, 1 medium, chopped
- Salt, to taste
- Ginger, 1 inch piece, minced
- Cumin seeds, ½ tbsp.
- Black peppercorns, 5
- Garlic, 3 cloves, minced
- Coriander seeds, 1 tbsp.

ssssssssssssssssssssssssssssssssssssssssssss

Procedure:

Heat 1 tbsp. oil and 1 tbsp. onion, dried chili, garlic, peppercorns, cumin seeds, ginger, coriander seeds and cloves. Cook for 5 minutes.

Turn off the flame and add fennel seeds. Combine well.

Grind the contents until it forms a paste.

Add remaining onions in the remaining oil and cook for 5 minutes.

Add tomato puree and simmer for 5 minutes.

Add ground spice and turmeric powder. Mix well.

Add a few drops of water and mix.

Now add crabs and salt and coat well. Cover the lid and cook for 5 minutes.

Uncover and cook for an additional 10 minutes while stirring occasionally.

Serve hot with coriander leaves on top.

28) Chicken Do Pyaaza

As the name suggests, chicken do pyaaza (onions) uses extra onions compared to what is used in normal gravy. Onions have a slightly sweet flavor which gives this dish a light sweet and spicy taste.

Yield: 4

Cooking Time: 60 minutes

List of Ingredients:

- Chicken, 1 pound, cubed
- Fenugreek seeds, 1 tbsp.
- Tomatoes, 2, chopped
- Coriander powder, 1 tbsp.
- Onions, 2, chopped
- Cream, 3 tbsp.
- Garlic paste, 2 tsp.
- Ginger paste, 1 tsp.
- Ginger garlic paste, 2 ½ tsp.
- Red chili powder, 1 tbsp.
- Cumin powder, 1 tbsp.
- Ghee, 1 ½ tbsp.
- Turmeric powder, 1 tbsp.
- Yogurt, 1 small cup
- Salt, to taste
- Coriander leaves, 1 tbsp.
- Green chilies, 1 tbsp., chopped
- Mint leaves, 1 tbsp.

For the Garam Masala:

- Green cardamom powder, 1 tbsp.
- Cinnamon powder, 1 tbsp.
- Mace powder, 1 tbsp.
- Black cardamom powder, ¼ tsp.
- Clove powder, 1 tbsp.

sssssssssssssssssssssssssssssssssssssssssssss

Procedure:

To make garam masala, combine all the ingredients together and keep aside.

To prepare chicken marinate it with ginger paste, chili powder and garlic paste. Keep aside.

Puree tomatoes.

Heat ghee and add ginger garlic paste. Sauté for 30 seconds. Add onions and cook until brown.

Add tomato puree and season with salt.

Beat yogurt with red chili powder and turmeric powder. Stir this mixture in the puree and cook for 2 minutes.

Now add garam masala, cumin powder, coriander powder, chicken and water. Cook for 10 minutes.

In a small pan heat cream with green chilies, coriander leaves, and fenugreek seeds and mint leaves.

Transfer the cooked chicken on the serving bowl and spread the cream mixture. Serve immediately.

29) Murg Rezala

Murg rezala is a Bengali specialty. The curry is made with cashews, coconut and khoya with gives it a rich and creamy texture. The chicken on the other hand is cooked in yogurt and spices making murg rezala a combination of a slightly sweet, creamy and savory dish.

Yield: 8

Cooking Time: 60 minutes

List of Ingredients:

- Chicken, 1 pound, cubed
- White onions, 1 cup
- Khoya, 150 g
- Curd, 1 cup
- White pepper, ¼ tsp.
- Silver leaves, 2
- Salt, to taste
- Garlic, ½ tsp.
- Ginger, ½ tsp.
- Ghee, 2 tbsp.
- Green cardamom, 12
- Cashews, ½ cup
- Coconut, 3 tbsp., grated
- Mitha ittr, 2 drops
- Screw pine, 2 drops

sssssssssssssssssssssssssssssssssssssssssssss

Procedure:

Blanch chicken cubes in boiling water. Strain and set aside.

Take out the juice of garlic and ginger. Set aside.

Process onions, and set aside.

Process coconut and set aside.

Process cashews and set aside.

Add chicken cubes in a deep pan and add water, green cardamom and salt. Boil the mixture and then simmer on low flame.

Now add onion paste and extracted juices from ginger and garlic. Cook for 5-10 minutes or until the mixture dries.

Now add ghee.

Beat curd well and add in the mixture. Fry until dry.

Stir coconut and cashew paste and fry for an additional 5 minutes.

Now add white pepper and 1 cup water. Simmer for 5 minutes.

Remove the pan from stove and add mashed khoya, mitha ittr and screw pine. Combine well.

Spread cream and garnish with silver leaves.

Serve hot.

30) Sali Marghi

Sali marghi is an ancient Parsee dish. Sali is potato string which is deep fried and served alongside entrees. The chicken is cooked in tomato sauce and other spices and has a tangy and spice blend of flavors.

Yield: 4

Cooking Time: 50 minutes

List of Ingredients:

- Onions, 1 cup, chopped
- Garam masala, ½ tbsp.
- Tomato sauce, 1 ½ cup
- Salt, to taste
- Cumin powder, 1 ½ tbsp.
- Red chili powder, ½ tbsp.
- Chicken, 8-10 pieces
- Garlic paste, 2 tsp.
- Green chili, 1, chopped
- Ginger, 1 tbsp., chopped
- Turmeric powder, ¼ tbsp.
- Water
- Sali for serving
- Oil, 3 tbsp.

sssssssssssssssssssssssssssssssssssssssssssssss

Procedure:

Heat oil in a deep pan and add onions, garlic and ginger. Sauté until golden.

Add tomato sauce and cook for 5 minutes.

Add chili powder, garam masala, turmeric and green chilies. Cook until the mixture releases its oil.

Add chicken and season with salt. Combine well.

Stir water and cover the lid. Simmer on low flame for 20 minutes.

Add cumin powder and stir until the gravy turns thick.

Transfer to serving dish and serve with Sali on top.

About the Author

Allie Allen developed her passion for the culinary arts at the tender age of five when she would help her mother cook for their large family of 8. Even back then, her family knew this would be more than a hobby for the young Allie and when she graduated from high school, she applied to cooking school in London. It had always been a dream of the young chef to study with some of Europe's best and she made it happen by attending the Chef Academy of London.

After graduation, Allie decided to bring her skills back to North America and open up her own restaurant. After 10 successful years as head chef and owner, she decided to sell her business and pursue other career avenues. This monumental decision led Allie to her true calling, teaching. She also started to write e-books for her students to study at home for practice. She is now the proud author of several e-books and gives private and semi-private cooking lessons to a range of students at all levels of experience.

Stay tuned for more from this dynamic chef and teacher when she releases more informative e-books on cooking and baking in the near future. Her work is infused with stores and anecdotes you will love!

Author's Afterthoughts

I can't tell you how grateful I am that you decided to read my book. My most heartfelt thanks that you took time out of your life to choose my work and I hope you find benefit within these pages.

There are so many books available today that offer similar content so that makes it even more humbling that you decided to buying mine.

Tell me what you thought! I am eager to hear your opinion and ideas on what you read as are others who are looking for a good book to buy. Leave a review on Amazon.com so others can benefit from your wisdom!

With much thanks,

Allie Allen

Printed in Great Britain
by Amazon